THIS BOOK BELONGS TO

Caroline arbogast

START DATE

11/16/22

SHE READS TRUTH

EXECUTIVE

FOUNDER/CHIEF EXECUTIVE OFFICER
Raechel Myers

CO-FOUNDER/CHIEF CONTENT OFFICER
Amanda Bible Williams

CHIEF OPERATING OFFICER/
CREATIVE DIRECTOR
Ryan Myers

EXECUTIVE ASSISTANT
Catherine Cromer

EDITORIAL

CONTENT DIRECTOR
John Greco, MDiv

MANAGING EDITOR
Jessica Lamb

PRODUCT MANAGER, KIDS READ TRUTH
Melanie Rainer, MATS

CONTENT EDITOR
Kara Gause

ASSOCIATE EDITOR
Ellen Taylor

CREATIVE

LEAD DESIGNER
Kelsea Allen

ARTIST IN RESIDENCE
Emily Knapp

DESIGNERS
Abbey Benson
Davis DeLisi

MARKETING

MARKETING DIRECTOR
Casey Campbell

SOCIAL MEDIA STRATEGIST
Ansley Rushing

PARTNERSHIP SPECIALIST
Kamiren Passavanti

COMMUNITY SUPPORT SPECIALIST
Margot Williams

SHIPPING & LOGISTICS

LOGISTICS MANAGER
Lauren Gloyne

SHIPPING MANAGER
Sydney Bess

FULFILLMENT COORDINATOR
Katy McKnight

FULFILLMENT SPECIALISTS
Sam Campos
Julia Rogers

SUBSCRIPTION INQUIRIES
orders@shereadstruth.com

CONTRIBUTORS

COVER PHOTOGRAPHER
Katie Lauritzen

PHOTOGRAPHERS
Katie Lauritzen (22, 47, 63)
Julia Madden Sears (10, 31, 54, 79, 91)

@SHEREADSTRUTH

Download the
She Reads Truth app,
available for iOS
and Android.

SHEREADSTRUTH.COM

This book was printed offset in Nashville, Tennessee, on 70# Lynx Opaque. Cover is 100# Cougar Opaque with a soft touch lamination.

GALATIANS

We care not only about
reading the Bible every day,
but also about understanding
it as we go.

Raechel Myers
FOUNDER & CHIEF
EXECUTIVE OFFICER

W hen I receive a letter in the mail (or, let's be honest: an email), I read it all at once. When Adele releases a new album, I eagerly listen to every track. When I make a sandwich (always with crispy iceberg lettuce), I eat the whole thing.

Isn't it a bit weird to read one of the most important letters of all time over the course of twenty-one days? It feels like we may be missing some big-picture ideas when we don't read the whole thing at once.

I read the book of Galatians this afternoon. It took me twenty-four minutes. That included the time it took to field a text from my sister, enjoy a venti tea and a cake pop from Starbucks, dig for a pencil so I could mark something that stood out to me, and reread a couple of paragraphs for understanding.

Twenty-four minutes isn't a lot of time. Google tells me the average (undistracted) reader can do it in about seventeen minutes. So why break it up across three weeks?

At She Reads Truth, we care not only about reading the Bible every day (and, boy, do we care about that!), but also about understanding it as we go. So when we come across a letter like Paul's epistle to the Galatians, we think it's a good idea to treat it, well, like a letter. Begin by reading the whole thing all at once. Then—once you have that big-picture idea of what Paul is trying to communicate to the church in Galatia—we can dig deeper, exploring the two covenants in Galatians 4, comparing the fruit of the Spirit with the works of the flesh, and hearing Paul's charge to "not get tired of doing good" (Gl 6:9).

We're excited that you're reading Paul's letter to the Galatians with us. And we really do want you to do some homework! Flip forward to page 16 and you'll find a reader's edition of the letter Paul wrote, free of verse markers, chapter breaks, and section headings (those were all added later). Once you've finished, you'll be all the more equipped to use this Study Book as it was designed to be used. And, more importantly, by the power of the very Spirit that Paul writes about, you will grow in your understanding of the foundational words that shaped, guarded, and encouraged the early Church.

May I recommend a nice cup of tea and a cake pop while you read?

DESIGN ON PURPOSE

Terrazzo tile is made by embedding marble, granite, quartz, or glass chips in a cement binder. The terrazzo in this book serves as a visual reminder of Paul's message in Galatians: a shared faith in Jesus brings diverse people together in His Church.

The use of the large, mixed-case font Plantin on the cover and in select places in the book emphasizes the harmony that comes when unlike things are unified by a common purpose.

Orange and blue are complementary colors on the color wheel, meaning they are a high-contrast pair. We chose these colors to highlight the struggle and tension that existed in the early Church as first-century followers of Jesus worked out what it means to be followers of Christ.

She Reads Truth is a community of women dedicated to reading the Word of God every day.

The Bible is living and active, breathed out by God, and we confidently hold it higher than anything we can do or say. This book focuses primarily on Scripture, with bonus resources to facilitate deeper engagement with God's Word.

SCRIPTURE READING

Designed for a Monday start, this Study Book presents the book of Galatians in daily readings, with supplemental passages for additional context.

JOURNALING SPACE

Each weekday features space for personal reflection and prayer.

GRACE DAY

Use Saturdays to pray, rest, and reflect on what you've read.

WEEKLY TRUTH

Sundays are set aside for weekly Scripture memorization.

Find the corresponding memory cards in the back of this book.

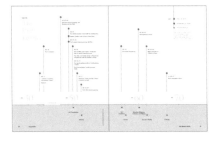

EXTRAS

This book features additional tools to help you gain a deeper understanding of the text.

PLANS

3 Weeks

Galatians

PLAN OVERVIEW

The book of Galatians is one of the apostle Paul's earliest and most passionate letters. In response to false teaching about what it takes to be part of the family of God, Paul wrote this letter to point believers to the truth of the gospel: our righteousness comes from the crucified Savior alone, not through anything we can do ourselves. Join us as we spend three weeks in Galatians, reading together about the freedom, goodness, and grace available through the gospel of Jesus Christ.

For added community and conversation, join us in the **Galatians** reading plan on the She Reads Truth app or at SheReadsTruth.com.

Contents

EXTRAS

She Reads Galatians	12
How to Read a New Testament Letter	14
Paul's Letter to the Galatians	16
Hymn: Blessed Assurance	24
The Mark of God's People	34

Timeline: Pauline Epistles	56
Recipe: Creamy Coconut Milk Chai	66
The Fruit of the Spirit	86
For the Record	104

WEEK 1

DAY 1	Greeting	19
DAY 2	No Other Gospel	22
DAY 3	Paul Defends His Apostleship	27
DAY 4	Paul Defends His Gospel at Jerusalem	30
DAY 5	Freedom from the Law	37
DAY 6	Grace Day	40
DAY 7	Weekly Truth	42
WEEK 1	Response Questions	44

WEEK 2

DAY 8	Justification Through Faith	46
DAY 9	Law and Promise	51
DAY 10	The Purpose of the Law	54
DAY 11	Sons and Heirs	59
DAY 12	Paul's Concern for the Galatians	62
DAY 13	Grace Day	68
DAY 14	Weekly Truth	70
WEEK 2	Response Questions	72

WEEK 3

DAY 15	Sarah and Hagar: Two Covenants	75
DAY 16	Freedom of the Christian	78
DAY 17	The Spirit Versus the Flesh	83
DAY 18	Carry One Another's Burdens	88
DAY 19	Concluding Exhortation	90
DAY 20	Grace Day	94
DAY 21	Weekly Truth	96
WEEK 3	Response Questions	98

I do not set aside the grace of God, for if righteousness comes through the law, then Christ died for nothing.

■ KEY VERSE GALATIANS 2:21

ON THE TIMELINE

A LITTLE BACKGROUND

No definite date can be determined for the writing of Galatians. The possible dates range from AD 48, since there is no mention of the Jerusalem Council (Ac 15), to AD 52 or 53, if shortly after Paul's second missionary journey, to AD 56, if written around the same time as the book of Romans during his third missionary journey.

The term *Galatians* was used both ethnically and politically in the New Testament era, making it unclear where the Galatian churches were actually located. If understood ethnically, the founding of the Galatian churches is only implied in the New Testament. Paul "went through the region of Phrygia and Galatia" (Ac 16:6), in north central Asia Minor, during his second missionary journey and again later (Ac 18:23; 19:1). A group from Gaul (modern France) invaded that area in the third century BC, and it became known as Galatia.

Understood politically, *Galatians* can refer to those living in the southern part of the Roman province of Galatia, a different area entirely. That region included the cities of Pisidian Antioch, Iconium, Lystra, and Derbe, where Paul worked to plant churches (Ac 13:14–14:23).

MESSAGE & PURPOSE

GIVE THANKS FOR THE BOOK OF GALATIANS

Galatians, which may be the earliest of Paul's letters, is also his most intense, proclaiming the truth that sinners are justified and live godly lives by trusting in Jesus alone. Paul wrote Galatians to clarify and defend "the truth of the gospel" (Gl 2:5, 16) in the face of a false gospel. He did this by defending his authority as an apostle, considering the Old Testament basis of the gospel message, and demonstrating how the gospel message worked practically in daily Christian living.

Galatians teaches extensively about the ministry of the Holy Spirit in relation to the Christian life. After the Spirit's role in the ministry of adoption (Gl 4:5–6), believers are commanded to "walk by the Spirit" (Gl 5:16), be "led by the Spirit" (Gl 5:18), and "keep in step with the Spirit" (Gl 5:25), as well as sow to the Spirit and reap the related eternal harvest (Gl 6:8). The moment-by-moment outcome of that kind of sensitivity to the ministry of the Holy Spirit is what is meant by "the fruit of the Spirit" (Gl 5:22–23).

How to Read a New Testament Letter

Most of the books that make up the New Testament are letters. These letters, also called *epistles*, come in a variety of shapes and sizes. Many are considered lengthy by ancient standards. Some were addressed to churches, while others were written to individuals. Some have been passed down to us with a name borrowed from their recipients, while others are known by their author.

HERE ARE SOME PRINCIPLES TO KEEP IN MIND AS YOU READ GALATIANS AND OTHER NEW TESTAMENT LETTERS:

READING A LETTER CAN BE LIKE LISTENING TO ONE SIDE OF A CONVERSATION.

1 Because we don't always know what specific questions or situations a writer was addressing, we must look for context clues in the letter to figure out what was going on.

LETTERS WERE MEANT TO BE READ ALL AT ONCE.

2 While there's nothing wrong with studying a particular passage or even a single verse, ancient letters, like the letters we write today, were meant to be read in a single sitting. Doing so allows the reader to see the author's progression of thought and make connections that might otherwise be missed.

THE NEW TESTAMENT LETTERS WERE WRITTEN TO BELIEVERS LEARNING TO LIVE IN CHRISTIAN COMMUNITY.

3 With a few exceptions (1 & 2 Timothy, Titus, Philemon, and 3 John), the letters in the New Testament were written to churches—groups of people who were learning to live as the people of God. When you see "you" in these letters, it's usually plural. These letters were typically read out loud so all could hear. They were even shared between congregations (Col 4:16).

INSTRUCTIONS WERE OFTEN TAILORED FOR A SPECIFIC AUDIENCE.

(4)

Not every instruction is meant to be applied by readers today. Some bits of guidance were written to counter a specific problem or abuse, while others articulate principles that are universally true.

NEW TESTAMENT LETTERS DRAW HEAVILY ON THE OLD TESTAMENT.

(5)

The Old Testament was the Bible of the early Church. Because it is "profitable for teaching, for rebuking, for correcting, [and] for training in righteousness" (2Tm 3:16), it was rightly applied to situations of all kinds. The better we know the Old Testament, the better equipped we will be to understand the New Testament letters.

THE NEW TESTAMENT LETTERS WERE ALL WRITTEN TO PEOPLE LEARNING TO FOLLOW CHRIST.

(6)

Whether Jewish or Gentile believers, the recipients of the New Testament letters had been rescued from the kingdom of darkness (Col 1:13). Nearly everything they thought they knew about the world and their place in it changed as a result of their entrance into God's kingdom. This new life came with its share of spiritual attacks, persecution, and mistakes. We read these letters today as fellow citizens who also have room to grow.

THE NEW TESTAMENT LETTERS ARE PART OF OUR FAMILY HISTORY.

(7)

These letters make up some of the earliest records we have of the Church. Much has changed in the last two thousand years, but the faith that brought hope to Christians in the Greco-Roman world is the same faith we hold on to today. Despite differences in culture, education, and language, we have much in common with the original recipients of the New Testament letters, namely the love of Jesus Christ.

JESUS IS THE POINT.

(8)

Though the New Testament letters were written years after Jesus's life, death, and resurrection, each and every one is about Him. These documents were penned so that readers would grow in their understanding of who He is, what He has done, and what He has promised to do, and in so doing, become more like Him.

GaLaTiAnS

The book of Galatians is a letter, meant to be read all at once. Take some time before you begin your daily reading to read through Galatians in one sitting, tracing Paul's progression of thought through the whole book before engaging individual sections.

To him be the glory forever
and ever. Amen.

GALATIANS 1:5

01 Greeting

WEEK 1

WEEK 2

WEEK 3

Galatians 1:1–5

GREETING

[1] Paul, an apostle—not from men or by man, but by Jesus Christ and God the Father who raised him from the dead— [2] and all the brothers who are with me:

To the churches of Galatia.

[3] Grace to you and peace from God the Father and our Lord Jesus Christ, [4] who gave himself for our sins to rescue us from this present evil age, according to the will of our God and Father. [5] To him be the glory forever and ever. Amen.

Psalm 16:1–11

CONFIDENCE IN THE LORD

A Miktam of David.

[1] Protect me, God, for I take refuge in you.

[2] I said to the LORD, "You are my Lord; I have nothing good besides you."

[3] As for the holy people who are in the land,
they are the noble ones.
All my delight is in them.
[4] The sorrows of those who take another god
for themselves will multiply;
I will not pour out their drink offerings of blood,
and I will not speak their names with my lips.

[5] LORD, you are my portion
and my cup of blessing;
you hold my future.
[6] The boundary lines have fallen for me
in pleasant places;
indeed, I have a beautiful inheritance.

[7] I will bless the LORD who counsels me—
even at night when my thoughts trouble me.
[8] I always let the LORD guide me.
Because he is at my right hand,
I will not be shaken.

[9] Therefore my heart is glad
and my whole being rejoices;
my body also rests securely.
[10] For you will not abandon me to Sheol;
you will not allow your faithful one to see decay.
[11] You reveal the path of life to me;
in your presence is abundant joy;
at your right hand are eternal pleasures.

1 Corinthians 15:1–11

RESURRECTION ESSENTIAL TO THE GOSPEL

[1] Now I want to make clear for you, brothers and sisters, the gospel I preached to you, which you received, on which you have taken your stand [2] and by which you are being saved, if you hold to the message I preached to you—unless you believed in vain. [3] For I passed on to you as most important what I also received: that Christ died for our sins according to the Scriptures, [4] that he was buried, that he was raised on the third day according to the Scriptures, [5] and that he appeared to Cephas, then to the Twelve. [6] Then he appeared to over five hundred brothers and sisters at one time; most of them are still alive, but some have fallen asleep. [7] Then he appeared to James, then to all the apostles. [8] Last of all, as to one born at the wrong time, he also appeared to me.

[9] For I am the least of the apostles, not worthy to be called an apostle, because I persecuted the church of God. [10] But by the grace of God I am what I am, and his grace toward me was not in vain. On the contrary, I worked harder than any of them, yet not I, but the grace of God that was with me. [11] Whether, then, it is I or they, so we proclaim and so you have believed.

Colossians 1:9–14

PRAYER FOR SPIRITUAL GROWTH

[9] For this reason also, since the day we heard this, we haven't stopped praying for you. We are asking that you may be filled with the knowledge of his will in all wisdom and spiritual understanding, [10] so that you may walk worthy of the Lord, fully pleasing to him: bearing fruit in every good work and growing in the knowledge of God, [11] being strengthened with all power, according to his glorious might, so that you may have great endurance and patience, joyfully [12] giving thanks to the Father, who has enabled you to share in the saints' inheritance in the light. [13] He has rescued us from the domain of darkness and transferred us into the kingdom of the Son he loves. [14] In him we have redemption, the forgiveness of sins.

02 No Other Gospel

WEEK 1

Galatians 1:6–10

NO OTHER GOSPEL

handwritten: STOP WORSHIPPING
1. music artists
2. satan
3. stars on the red carpet etc.
who are we worshiping?

⁶ I am amazed that you are so quickly turning away from him who called you by the grace of Christ and are turning to a different gospel— ⁷ not that there is another gospel, but there are some who are troubling you and want to distort the gospel of Christ. ⁸ But even if we or an angel from heaven should preach to you a gospel contrary to what we have preached to you, a curse be on him! ⁹ As we have said before, I now say again: If anyone is preaching to you a gospel contrary to what you received, a curse be on him!

handwritten: they don't want you to know the good news

handwritten: said twice: important

¹⁰ For am I now trying to persuade people, or God? Or am I striving to please people? If I were still trying to please people, I would not be a servant of Christ.

handwritten: stop people pleasing, please Christ this is who matters.

WEEK 2

WEEK 3

Study questions on p. 44

Isaiah 52:1–10

[1] "Wake up, wake up;
put on your strength, Zion! *Ruler?*
Put on your beautiful garments,
Jerusalem, the Holy City!
For the uncircumcised and the unclean
will no longer enter you. *new times*

[2] **Stand up, shake the dust off yourself!** *amazing reminder!*

Take your seat, Jerusalem.
Remove the bonds from your neck,
captive Daughter Zion."
[3] For this is what the LORD says:
"You were sold for nothing,
and you will be redeemed without silver."
[4] For this is what the Lord GOD says:
"At first my people went down to Egypt to reside there,
then Assyria oppressed them without cause. *The Lord always has a plan*
[5] So now what have I here"—
   this is the LORD's declaration—
"that my people are taken away for nothing?
Its rulers wail"—
   this is the LORD's declaration—
"and my name is continually blasphemed all day long.
[6] Therefore my people will know my name;
therefore they will know on that day
that I am he who says: *The Lord is > than all of everything.*
Here I am."

[7] How beautiful on the mountains
are the feet of the herald,
who proclaims peace,
who brings news of good things,
who proclaims salvation, *Jesus saves people everyday*
who says to Zion, "Your God reigns!"
[8] The voices of your watchmen—
they lift up their voices,
shouting for joy together;
for every eye will see
when the LORD returns to Zion.

[9] Be joyful, rejoice together,
you ruins of Jerusalem!
For the LORD has comforted his people;
he has redeemed Jerusalem.
[10] The LORD has displayed his holy arm
in the sight of all the nations;
all the ends of the earth will see
the salvation of our God.

God always makes happy endings, no matter what we have to endure to get there!!

2 Corinthians 11:1–4, 12–15

PAUL AND THE FALSE APOSTLES

[1] I wish you would put up with a little foolishness from me. Yes, do put up with me! [2] For I am jealous for you with a godly jealousy, because I have promised you in marriage to one husband—to present a pure virgin to Christ. [3] But I fear that, as the serpent deceived Eve by his cunning, your minds may be seduced from a sincere and pure devotion to Christ. [4] For if a person comes and preaches another Jesus, whom we did not preach, or you receive a different spirit, which you had not received, or a different gospel, which you had not accepted, you put up with it splendidly!

…

[12] But I will continue to do what I am doing, in order to deny an opportunity to those who want to be regarded as our equals in what they boast about. [13] For such people are false apostles, deceitful workers, disguising themselves as apostles of Christ. [14] And no wonder! For Satan disguises himself as an angel of light. [15] So it is no great surprise if his servants also disguise themselves as servants of righteousness. Their end will be according to their works.

we ♥ Jesus but the sly satan can feel like it's around more.

If satan can disguise his works, we can do it even easier as humans on earth.

Takeaways
• Trust God through every step
• Be yourself through Christ
• God is > than everything
• Worship Him always.

Blessed Assurance

Blessed assurance, Jesus is mine!
O what a foretaste of glory divine!
Heir of salvation, purchase of God,
born of His Spirit, washed in His blood.

This is my story, this is my song,
praising my Savior all the day long;
This is my story, this is my song,
praising my Savior all the day long.

Perfect submission, perfect delight,
visions of rapture now burst on my sight;
Angels descending, bring from above
echoes of mercy, whispers of love.

This is my story, this is my song,
praising my Savior all the day long;
This is my story, this is my song,
praising my Savior all the day long.

Perfect submission, all is at rest,
I in my Savior am happy and blest,
watching and waiting, looking above,
filled with His goodness, lost in His love.

This is my story, this is my song,
praising my Savior all the day long;
This is my story, this is my song,
praising my Savior all the day long.

TUNE
Phoebe P. Knapp, 1873

TEXT
Fanny J. Crosby, 1873

1 Bles-sed as - su - rance, Je - sus is mine! O what a fore - taste of
2 Per - fect sub - mis - sion, per - fect de - light, vi - sions of rap - ture now
3 Per - fect sub - mis - sion, all is at rest, I in my Sa - vior am

glo - ry di - vine! Heir of sal - va - tion, pur - chase of God,
burst on my sight; An - gels des - cen - ding, bring from a - bove
hap - py and blest, watch - ing and wait - ing, look - ing a - bove,

Refrain

born of His Spi - rit, washed in His blood. This is my sto - ry,
e - choes of mer - cy, whis - pers of love.
filled with His good - ness, lost in His love.

this is my song, prais - ing my Sa - vior all the day long; This is my

sto - ry, this is my song, prais - ing my Sa - vior all the day long.

For I want you to know,
brothers and sisters, that the
gospel preached by me is not
of human origin.

GALATIANS 1:11

03 Paul Defends His Apostleship

● WEEK 1

○ WEEK 2

○ WEEK 3

Galatians 1:11–24

PAUL DEFENDS HIS APOSTLESHIP

[11] For I want you to know, brothers and sisters, that the gospel preached by me is not of human origin. [12] For I did not receive it from a human source and I was not taught it, but it came by a revelation of Jesus Christ.

[13] For you have heard about my former way of life in Judaism: I intensely persecuted God's church and tried to destroy it. [14] I advanced in Judaism beyond many contemporaries among my people, because I was extremely zealous for the traditions of my ancestors. [15] But when God, who from my mother's womb set me apart and called me by his grace, was pleased [16] to reveal his Son in me, so that I could preach him among the Gentiles, I did not immediately consult with anyone. [17] I did not go up to Jerusalem to those who had become apostles before me; instead I went to Arabia and came back to Damascus.

[18] Then after three years I did go up to Jerusalem to get to know Cephas, and I stayed with him fifteen days. [19] But I didn't see any of the other apostles except James, the Lord's brother. [20] I declare in the sight of God: I am not lying in what I write to you.

[21] Afterward, I went to the regions of Syria and Cilicia. [22] I remained personally unknown to the Judean churches that are in Christ. [23] They simply kept hearing: "He who formerly persecuted us now preaches the faith he once tried to destroy." [24] And they glorified God because of me.

Joel 2:12–14

GOD'S CALL FOR REPENTANCE

[12] Even now—

this is the LORD's declaration—
turn to me with all your heart,
with fasting, weeping, and mourning.
[13] Tear your hearts,
not just your clothes,
and return to the LORD your God.
For he is gracious and compassionate,
slow to anger, abounding in faithful love,
and he relents from sending disaster.
[14] Who knows? He may turn and relent
and leave a blessing behind him,
so you can offer grain and wine
to the LORD your God.

Acts 9:1–22

THE DAMASCUS ROAD

[1] Now Saul was still breathing threats and murder against the disciples of the Lord. He went to the high priest [2] and requested letters from him to the synagogues in Damascus, so that if he found any men or women who belonged to the Way, he might bring them as prisoners to Jerusalem. [3] As he traveled and was nearing Damascus, a light from heaven suddenly flashed around him. [4] Falling to the ground, he heard a voice saying to him, "Saul, Saul, why are you persecuting me?"

[5] "Who are you, Lord?" Saul said.

"I am Jesus, the one you are persecuting," he replied. [6] "But get up and go into the city, and you will be told what you must do."

[7] The men who were traveling with him stood speechless, hearing the sound but seeing no one. [8] Saul got up from the ground, and though his eyes were open, he could see nothing. So they took him by the hand and led him into Damascus. [9] He was unable to see for three days and did not eat or drink.

SAUL'S BAPTISM

[10] There was a disciple in Damascus named Ananias, and the Lord said to him in a vision, "Ananias."

"Here I am, Lord," he replied.

[11] "Get up and go to the street called Straight," the Lord said to him, "to the house of Judas, and ask for a man from Tarsus named Saul, since he is praying there. [12] In a vision he has seen a man named Ananias coming in and placing his hands on him so that he may regain his sight."

[13] "Lord," Ananias answered, "I have heard from many people about this man, how much harm he has done to your saints in Jerusalem. [14] And he has authority here from the chief priests to arrest all who call on your name."

[15] But the Lord said to him, "Go, for this man is my chosen instrument to take my name to Gentiles, kings, and Israelites. [16] I will show him how much he must suffer for my name."

[17] Ananias went and entered the house. He placed his hands on him and said, "Brother Saul, the Lord Jesus, who appeared to you on the road you were traveling, has sent me so that you may regain your sight and be filled with the Holy Spirit."

[18] At once something like scales fell from his eyes, and he regained his sight. Then he got up and was baptized. [19] And after taking some food, he regained his strength.

SAUL PROCLAIMING THE MESSIAH

Saul was with the disciples in Damascus for some time. [20] Immediately he began proclaiming Jesus in the synagogues: "He is the Son of God."

[21] All who heard him were astounded and said, "Isn't this the man in Jerusalem who was causing havoc for those who called on this name and came here for the purpose of taking them as prisoners to the chief priests?"

[22] But Saul grew stronger and kept confounding the Jews who lived in Damascus by proving that Jesus is the Messiah.

04 Paul Defends His Gospel at Jerusalem

● WEEK 1

○ WEEK 2

○ WEEK 3

Galatians 2:1–10

PAUL DEFENDS HIS GOSPEL AT JERUSALEM

[1] Then after fourteen years I went up again to Jerusalem with Barnabas, taking Titus along also. [2] I went up according to a revelation and presented to them the gospel I preach among the Gentiles, but privately to those recognized as leaders. I wanted to be sure I was not running, and had not been running, in vain. [3] But not even Titus, who was with me, was compelled to be circumcised, even though he was a Greek. [4] This matter arose because some false brothers had infiltrated our ranks to spy on the freedom we have in Christ Jesus in order to enslave us. [5] But we did not give up and submit to these people for even a moment, so that the truth of the gospel would be preserved for you.

[6] Now from those recognized as important (what they once were makes no difference to me; God does not show favoritism)—they added nothing to me. [7] On the contrary, they saw that I had been entrusted with the gospel for the uncircumcised, just as Peter was for the circumcised, [8] since the one at work in Peter for an apostleship to the circumcised was also at work in me for the Gentiles. [9] When James, Cephas, and John—those recognized as pillars—acknowledged the grace that had been given to me, they gave the right hand of fellowship to me and Barnabas, agreeing that we should go to the Gentiles and they to the circumcised. [10] They asked only that we would remember the poor, which I had made every effort to do.

But we did not give up and submit
to these people for even a moment,
so that the truth of the gospel would
be preserved for you.

GALATIANS 2:5

Isaiah 19:21–25

²¹ The Lᴏʀᴅ will make himself known to Egypt, and Egypt will know the Lᴏʀᴅ on that day. They will offer sacrifices and offerings; they will make vows to the Lᴏʀᴅ and fulfill them. ²² The Lᴏʀᴅ will strike Egypt, striking and healing. Then they will turn to the Lᴏʀᴅ and he will be receptive to their prayers and heal them.

²³ On that day there will be a highway from Egypt to Assyria. Assyria will go to Egypt, Egypt to Assyria, and Egypt will worship with Assyria.

²⁴ On that day Israel will form a triple alliance with Egypt and Assyria—a blessing within the land. ²⁵ The Lᴏʀᴅ of Armies will bless them, saying, "Egypt my people, Assyria my handiwork, and Israel my inheritance are blessed."

Acts 15:1–29

DISPUTE IN ANTIOCH

¹ Some men came down from Judea and began to teach the brothers: "Unless you are circumcised according to the custom prescribed by Moses, you cannot be saved." ² After Paul and Barnabas had engaged them in serious argument and debate, Paul and Barnabas and some others were appointed to go up to the apostles and elders in Jerusalem about this issue. ³ When they had been sent on their way by the church, they passed through both Phoenicia and Samaria, describing in detail the conversion of the Gentiles, and they brought great joy to all the brothers and sisters.

⁴ When they arrived at Jerusalem, they were welcomed by the church, the apostles, and the elders, and they reported all that God had done with them. ⁵ But some of the believers who belonged to the party of the Pharisees stood up and said, "It is necessary to circumcise them and to command them to keep the law of Moses."

THE JERUSALEM COUNCIL

⁶ The apostles and the elders gathered to consider this matter. ⁷ After there had been much debate, Peter stood up and said to them: "Brothers and sisters, you are aware that in the early days God made a choice among you, that by my mouth the Gentiles would hear the gospel message and believe. ⁸ And God, who knows the heart, bore witness to them by giving them the Holy Spirit, just as he also did to us. ⁹ He made no distinction between us and them, cleansing their hearts by faith. ¹⁰ Now then, why are you testing God by putting a yoke on the disciples' necks that neither our ancestors nor we have been able to bear? ¹¹ On the contrary, we believe that we are saved through the grace of the Lord Jesus in the same way they are."

¹² The whole assembly became silent and listened to Barnabas and Paul describe all the signs and wonders God had done through them among the Gentiles.

¹³ After they stopped speaking, James responded: "Brothers and sisters, listen to me. ¹⁴ Simeon has reported how God first intervened to take from the Gentiles a people for his name. ¹⁵ And the words of the prophets agree with this, as it is written:

¹⁶ After these things I will return
and rebuild David's fallen tent.
I will rebuild its ruins
and set it up again,
¹⁷ so the rest of humanity
may seek the Lord—
even all the Gentiles
who are called by my name—
declares the Lord
who makes these things ¹⁸ known from long ago.

¹⁹ Therefore, in my judgment, we should not cause difficulties for those among the Gentiles who turn to God, ²⁰ but instead we should write to them to abstain from things polluted by idols, from sexual immorality, from eating anything that has been strangled, and from blood. ²¹ For since ancient times, Moses has had those who proclaim him in every city, and every Sabbath day he is read aloud in the synagogues."

THE LETTER TO THE GENTILE BELIEVERS

²² Then the apostles and the elders, with the whole church, decided to select men who were among them and to send them to Antioch with Paul and Barnabas: Judas, called Barsabbas, and Silas, both leading men among the brothers. ²³ They wrote:

"From the apostles and the elders, your brothers,

To the brothers and sisters among the Gentiles in Antioch, Syria, and Cilicia:

Greetings.

²⁴ Since we have heard that some without our authorization went out from us and troubled you with their words and unsettled your hearts, ²⁵ we have unanimously decided to select men and send them to you along with our dearly loved Barnabas and Paul, ²⁶ who have risked their lives for the name of our Lord Jesus Christ. ²⁷ Therefore we have sent Judas and Silas, who will personally report the same things by word of mouth. ²⁸ For it was the Holy Spirit's decision—and ours—not to place further burdens on you beyond these requirements: ²⁹ that you abstain from food offered to idols, from blood, from eating anything that has been strangled, and from sexual immorality. You will do well if you keep yourselves from these things.

Farewell."

THE MARK OF GOD'S PEOPLE

Much of Paul's letter to the Galatians deals with the issue of circumcision. Certain false teachers were attempting to convince the Galatian Christians they needed to be circumcised to be true followers of Christ. Understanding the Old Testament cultural background of circumcision helps us better appreciate to the Galatians' dilemma and Paul's fierce response.

"My covenant will be marked in your flesh as a permanent covenant."

GENESIS 17:13

In the book of Genesis, God promised to make Abraham's descendants into a great nation, one formed in the womb of a barren woman beyond childbearing age (Gn 17:1–8, 17–19). As a reminder of their miraculous origins as a people and a sign of the covenant God made with Abraham, every male was to bear the mark of circumcision (Gn 17:12–14).

And if you belong to Christ, then you are Abraham's seed, heirs according to the promise.

GALATIANS 3:29

The Galatians understood that in Christ, they were now a part of Abraham's family and the recipients of God's promise to bless all nations (Gn 18:18; 22:18). The false teachers in their midst argued it must also be necessary to have the sign of the covenant (circumcision) to show they, too, were included within the community of God's people (Gl 2:2–4; 6:12).

If anyone is preaching to you a gospel contrary to what you received, a curse be on him!

GALATIANS 1:9

Paul saw through this faulty reasoning, and he reminded the Christians in Galatia that Jesus has already provided everything necessary to be brought into God's family—to be saved, forgiven, and made new (Gl 3:11–14). Anything we might want to add to this truth is an affront to the sufficiency of Christ and an outright rejection of the gospel itself (Gl 1:6–9). It is faith that saves, not circumcision or any other deed we can perform, no matter how good or how costly (Gl 2:16).

I have been crucified with
Christ, and I no longer live,
but Christ lives in me.

GALATIANS 2:20

05 Freedom from the Law

WEEK 1

WEEK 2

WEEK 3

Galatians 2:11–21

FREEDOM FROM THE LAW

[11] But when Cephas came to Antioch, I opposed him to his face because he stood condemned. [12] For he regularly ate with the Gentiles before certain men came from James. However, when they came, he withdrew and separated himself, because he feared those from the circumcision party. [13] Then the rest of the Jews joined his hypocrisy, so that even Barnabas was led astray by their hypocrisy. [14] But when I saw that they were deviating from the truth of the gospel, I told Cephas in front of everyone, "If you, who are a Jew, live like a Gentile and not like a Jew, how can you compel Gentiles to live like Jews?"

[15] We are Jews by birth and not "Gentile sinners," [16] and yet because we know that a person is not justified by the works of the law but by faith in Jesus Christ, even we ourselves have believed in Christ Jesus. This was so that we might be justified by faith in Christ and not by the works of the law, because by the works of the law no human being will be justified. [17] But if we ourselves are also found to be "sinners" while seeking to be justified by Christ, is Christ then a promoter of sin? Absolutely not! [18] If I rebuild those things that I tore down, I show myself to be a lawbreaker. [19] For through the law I died to the law, so that I might live for God. [20] I have been crucified with Christ, and I no longer live, but Christ lives in me. The life I now live in the body, I live by faith in the Son of God, who loved me and gave himself for me. [21] I do not set aside the grace of God, for if righteousness comes through the law, then Christ died for nothing.

Deuteronomy 10:12–17

WHAT GOD REQUIRES

¹² "And now, Israel, what does the LORD your God ask of you except to fear the LORD your God by walking in all his ways, to love him, and to worship the LORD your God with all your heart and all your soul? ¹³ Keep the LORD's commands and statutes I am giving you today, for your own good. ¹⁴ The heavens, indeed the highest heavens, belong to the LORD your God, as does the earth and everything in it. ¹⁵ Yet the LORD had his heart set on your fathers and loved them. He chose their descendants after them—he chose you out of all the peoples, as it is today. ¹⁶ Therefore, circumcise your hearts and don't be stiff-necked any longer. ¹⁷ For the LORD your God is the God of gods and Lord of lords, the great, mighty, and awe-inspiring God, showing no partiality and taking no bribe."

Acts 10:9–48

PETER'S VISION

⁹ The next day, as they were traveling and nearing the city, Peter went up to pray on the roof about noon. ¹⁰ He became hungry and wanted to eat, but while they were preparing something, he fell into a trance. ¹¹ He saw heaven opened and an object that resembled a large sheet coming down, being lowered by its four corners to the earth. ¹² In it were all the four-footed animals and reptiles of the earth, and the birds of the sky. ¹³ A voice said to him, "Get up, Peter; kill and eat."

¹⁴ "No, Lord!" Peter said. "For I have never eaten anything impure and ritually unclean."

¹⁵ Again, a second time, the voice said to him, "What God has made clean, do not call impure." ¹⁶ This happened three times, and suddenly the object was taken up into heaven.

PETER VISITS CORNELIUS

¹⁷ While Peter was deeply perplexed about what the vision he had seen might mean, right away the men who had been sent by Cornelius, having asked directions to Simon's house, stood at the gate. ¹⁸ They called out, asking if Simon, who was also named Peter, was lodging there.

¹⁹ While Peter was thinking about the vision, the Spirit told him, "Three men are here looking for you. ²⁰ Get up, go downstairs, and go with them with no doubts at all, because I have sent them."

²¹ Then Peter went down to the men and said, "Here I am, the one you're looking for. What is the reason you're here?"

²² They said, "Cornelius, a centurion, an upright and God-fearing man, who has a good reputation with the whole Jewish nation, was divinely directed by a holy angel to call you to his house and to hear a message from you." ²³ Peter then invited them in and gave them lodging.

The next day he got up and set out with them, and some of the brothers from Joppa went with him. ²⁴ The following day he entered Caesarea. Now Cornelius was expecting them and had called together his relatives and close friends. ²⁵ When Peter entered, Cornelius met him, fell at his feet, and worshiped him.

²⁶ But Peter lifted him up and said, "Stand up. I myself am also a man." ²⁷ While talking with him, he went in and found a large gathering of people. ²⁸ Peter said to them, "You know it's forbidden for a Jewish man to associate with or visit a foreigner, but God has shown me that I must not call any person impure or unclean. ²⁹ That's why I came without any objection when I was sent for. So may I ask why you sent for me?"

³⁰ Cornelius replied, "Four days ago at this hour, at three in the afternoon, I was praying in my house. Just then a man in dazzling clothing stood before me ³¹ and said, 'Cornelius, your prayer has been heard, and your acts of charity have been remembered in God's sight. ³² Therefore send someone to Joppa and invite Simon here, who is also named Peter. He is lodging in Simon the tanner's house by the sea.' ³³ So I immediately sent for you, and it was good of you to come. So now we are all in the presence of God to hear everything you have been commanded by the Lord."

[34] Peter began to speak: "Now I truly understand that God doesn't show favoritism, [35] but in every nation the person who fears him and does what is right is acceptable to him. [36] He sent the message to the Israelites, proclaiming the good news of peace through Jesus Christ—he is Lord of all. [37] You know the events that took place throughout all Judea, beginning from Galilee after the baptism that John preached: [38] how God anointed Jesus of Nazareth with the Holy Spirit and with power, and how he went about doing good and healing all who were under the tyranny of the devil, because God was with him. [39] We ourselves are witnesses of everything he did in both the Judean country and in Jerusalem, and yet they killed him by hanging him on a tree. [40] God raised up this man on the third day and caused him to be seen, [41] not by all the people, but by us whom God appointed as witnesses, who ate and drank with him after he rose from the dead. [42] He commanded us to preach to the people and to testify that he is the one appointed by God to be the judge of the living and the dead. [43] All the prophets testify about him that through his name everyone who believes in him receives forgiveness of sins."

GENTILE CONVERSION AND BAPTISM

[44] While Peter was still speaking these words, the Holy Spirit came down on all those who heard the message. [45] The circumcised believers who had come with Peter were amazed because the gift of the Holy Spirit had been poured out even on the Gentiles. [46] For they heard them speaking in other tongues and declaring the greatness of God.

Then Peter responded, [47] "Can anyone withhold water and prevent these people from being baptized, who have received the Holy Spirit just as we have?" [48] He commanded them to be baptized in the name of Jesus Christ. Then they asked him to stay for a few days.

1 Corinthians 7:17–19

VARIOUS SITUATIONS OF LIFE

[17] Let each one live his life in the situation the Lord assigned when God called him. This is what I command in all the churches. [18] Was anyone already circumcised when he was called? He should not undo his circumcision. Was anyone called while uncircumcised? He should not get circumcised. [19] Circumcision does not matter and uncircumcision does not matter. Keeping God's commands is what matters.

 GRACE DAY

Use this day to pray, rest, and reflect on this week's reading, giving thanks for the grace that is ours in Christ.

He has rescued us from
the domain of darkness
and transferred us into the
kingdom of the Son he loves.
In him we have redemption,
the forgiveness of sins.

COLOSSIANS 1:13–14

07 WEEKLY TRUTH

Scripture is God-breathed and true. When we memorize it, we carry the gospel with us wherever we go.

This week we will memorize the key verse for Galatians.

Find the corresponding memory card in the back of this book.

WEEK 1

WEEK 2

WEEK 3

I do not set aside the grace of God, for if righteousness comes through the law, then Christ died for nothing.

GALATIANS 2:21

Response Questions

Galatians 1:6–10

NO OTHER GOSPEL

6 I am amazed that you are so quickly turning away from him who called you by the grace of Christ and are turning to a different gospel—7 not that there is another gospel, but there are some who are troubling you and want to distort the gospel of Christ. 8 But even if we or an angel from heaven should preach to you a gospel contrary to what we have preached to you, a curse be on him! 9 As we have said before, I now say again: If anyone is preaching to you a gospel contrary to what you received, a curse be on him!

10 For am I now trying to persuade people, or God? Or am I striving to please people? If I were still trying to please people, I would not be a servant of Christ.

1. Reflect on the passage. What was your immediate reaction upon reading it? Did anything stand out to you?

2. Paul writes that the Galatians are turning away from the gospel of Christ. What do you think Paul means by "turning to a different gospel"?

3. Do you ever find yourself working to please other people instead of God? How does that affect your relationship with God?

1) Cursed by God, **when you preach falsly**
Why would you please people when it hurts God.

2) Wether or not you deny God can be different for all
We don't know who is troubling us or if other people are being troubled.

3) Yes, trying to divide your time is impossible and you cannot do that.

08 Justification Through Faith

WEEK 1

WEEK 2

WEEK 3

Galatians 3:1–9

JUSTIFICATION THROUGH FAITH

[1] You foolish Galatians! Who has cast a spell on you, before whose eyes Jesus Christ was publicly portrayed as crucified? [2] I only want to learn this from you: Did you receive the Spirit by the works of the law or by believing what you heard? [3] Are you so foolish? After beginning by the Spirit, are you now finishing by the flesh? [4] Did you experience so much for nothing—if in fact it was for nothing? [5] So then, does God give you the Spirit and work miracles among you by your doing the works of the law? Or is it by believing what you heard— [6] just like Abraham who believed God, and it was credited to him for righteousness?

[7] You know, then, that those who have faith, these are Abraham's sons. [8] Now the Scripture saw in advance that God would justify the Gentiles by faith and proclaimed the gospel ahead of time to Abraham, saying, All the nations will be blessed through you. [9] Consequently those who have faith are blessed with Abraham, who had faith.

Genesis 15:1–6

THE ABRAHAMIC COVENANT

¹ After these events, the word of the LORD came to Abram in a vision:

> Do not be afraid, Abram.
> I am your shield;

your reward will be very great.

² But Abram said, "Lord GOD, what can you give me, since I am childless and the heir of my house is Eliezer of Damascus?" ³ Abram continued, "Look, you have given me no offspring, so a slave born in my house will be my heir."

⁴ Now the word of the LORD came to him: "This one will not be your heir; instead, one who comes from your own body will be your heir." ⁵ He took him outside and said, "Look at the sky and count the stars, if you are able to count them." Then he said to him, "Your offspring will be that numerous."

⁶ Abram believed the LORD, and he credited it to him as righteousness.

Matthew 3:1–12

THE HERALD OF THE CHRIST

¹ In those days John the Baptist came, preaching in the wilderness of Judea ² and saying, "Repent, because the kingdom of heaven has come near!" ³ For he is the one spoken of through the prophet Isaiah, who said:

> A voice of one crying out in the wilderness:
> Prepare the way for the Lord;
> make his paths straight!

⁴ Now John had a camel-hair garment with a leather belt around his waist, and his food was locusts and wild honey. ⁵ Then people from Jerusalem, all Judea, and all the vicinity of the Jordan were going out to him, ⁶ and they were baptized by him in the Jordan River, confessing their sins.

⁷ When he saw many of the Pharisees and Sadducees coming to his baptism, he said to them, "Brood of vipers! Who warned you to flee from the coming wrath? ⁸ Therefore produce fruit consistent with repentance. ⁹ And don't presume to say to yourselves, 'We have Abraham as our father.' For I tell you that God is able to raise up children for Abraham from these stones. ¹⁰ The ax is already at the root of the trees. Therefore, every tree that doesn't produce good fruit will be cut down and thrown into the fire.

[11] "I baptize you with water for repentance, but the one who is coming after me is more powerful than I. I am not worthy to remove his sandals. He himself will baptize you with the Holy Spirit and fire. [12] His winnowing shovel is in his hand, and he will clear his threshing floor and gather his wheat into the barn. But the chaff he will burn with fire that never goes out."

Romans 4:13–25

THE PROMISE GRANTED THROUGH FAITH

[13] For the promise to Abraham or to his descendants that he would inherit the world was not through the law, but through the righteousness that comes by faith. [14] If those who are of the law are heirs, faith is made empty and the promise nullified, [15] because the law produces wrath. And where there is no law, there is no transgression.

[16] This is why the promise is by faith, so that it may be according to grace, to guarantee it to all the descendants—not only to those who are of the law but also to those who are of Abraham's faith. He is the father of us all. [17] As it is written: I have made you the father of many nations. He is our father in God's sight, in whom Abraham believed—the God who gives life to the dead and calls things into existence that do not exist. [18] He believed, hoping against hope, so that he became the father of many nations according to what had been spoken: So will your descendants be. [19] He did not weaken in faith when he considered his own body to be already dead (since he was about a hundred years old) and also the deadness of Sarah's womb. [20] He did not waver in unbelief at God's promise but was strengthened in his faith and gave glory to God, [21] because he was fully convinced that what God had promised, he was also able to do. [22] Therefore, it was credited to him for righteousness. [23] Now it was credited to him was not written for Abraham alone, [24] but also for us. It will be credited to us who believe in him who raised Jesus our Lord from the dead. [25] He was delivered up for our trespasses and raised for our justification.

Christ redeemed us from the
curse of the law by becoming
a curse for us...

GALATIANS 3:13

09 Law and Promise

WEEK 1

WEEK 2

WEEK 3

Galatians 3:10–18

LAW AND PROMISE

¹⁰ For all who rely on the works of the law are under a curse, because it is written, Everyone who does not do everything written in the book of the law is cursed. ¹¹ Now it is clear that no one is justified before God by the law, because the righteous will live by faith. ¹² But the law is not based on faith; instead, the one who does these things will live by them. ¹³ Christ redeemed us from the curse of the law by becoming a curse for us, because it is written, Cursed is everyone who is hung on a tree. ¹⁴ The purpose was that the blessing of Abraham would come to the Gentiles by Christ Jesus, so that we could receive the promised Spirit through faith.

¹⁵ Brothers and sisters, I'm using a human illustration. No one sets aside or makes additions to a validated human will. ¹⁶ Now the promises were spoken to Abraham and to his seed. He does not say "and to seeds," as though referring to many, but referring to one, and to your seed, who is Christ. ¹⁷ My point is this: The law, which came 430 years later, does not invalidate a covenant previously established by God and thus cancel the promise. ¹⁸ For if the inheritance is based on the law, it is no longer based on the promise; but God has graciously given it to Abraham through the promise.

Genesis 12:1–7

THE CALL OF ABRAM

¹ The Lord said to Abram:

Go out from your land,
your relatives,
and your father's house
to the land that I will show you.
² I will make you into a great nation,
I will bless you,
I will make your name great,
and you will be a blessing.
³ I will bless those who bless you,
I will curse anyone who treats you with contempt,
and all the peoples on earth
will be blessed through you.

⁴ So Abram went, as the Lord had told him, and Lot went with him. Abram was seventy-five years old when he left Haran. ⁵ He took his wife Sarai, his nephew Lot, all the possessions they had accumulated, and the people they had acquired in Haran, and they set out for the land of Canaan. When they came to the land of Canaan, ⁶ Abram passed through the land to the site of Shechem, at the oak of Moreh. (At that time the Canaanites were in the land.) ⁷ The Lord appeared to Abram and said, "To your offspring I will give this land." So he built an altar there to the Lord who had appeared to him.

Isaiah 53:1–12

¹ Who has believed what we have heard?
And to whom has the arm of the Lord been revealed?
² He grew up before him like a young plant
and like a root out of dry ground.
He didn't have an impressive form
or majesty that we should look at him,
no appearance that we should desire him.
³ He was despised and rejected by men,
a man of suffering who knew what sickness was.
He was like someone people turned away from;
he was despised, and we didn't value him.

⁴ Yet he himself bore
 our sicknesses,
and he carried our pains;

but we in turn regarded him stricken,
struck down by God, and afflicted.
⁵ But he was pierced because of our rebellion,
crushed because of our iniquities;
punishment for our peace was on him,
and we are healed by his wounds.
⁶ We all went astray like sheep;
we all have turned to our own way;
and the Lord has punished him
for the iniquity of us all.

⁷ He was oppressed and afflicted,
yet he did not open his mouth.
Like a lamb led to the slaughter
and like a sheep silent before her shearers,
he did not open his mouth.
⁸ He was taken away because of oppression and judgment;
and who considered his fate?
For he was cut off from the land of the living;
he was struck because of my people's rebellion.
⁹ He was assigned a grave with the wicked,
but he was with a rich man at his death,
because he had done no violence
and had not spoken deceitfully.

¹⁰ Yet the Lord was pleased to crush him severely.
When you make him a guilt offering,
he will see his seed, he will prolong his days,
and by his hand, the Lord's pleasure will be accomplished.
¹¹ After his anguish,
he will see light and be satisfied.
By his knowledge,
my righteous servant will justify many,
and he will carry their iniquities.
¹² Therefore I will give him the many as a portion,
and he will receive the mighty as spoil,

because he willingly submitted to death,
and was counted among the rebels;
yet he bore the sin of many
and interceded for the rebels.

1 Peter 2:24–25

[24] He himself bore our sins in his body on the tree; so that, having died to sins, we might live for righteousness. By his wounds you have been healed. [25] For you were like sheep going astray, but you have now returned to the Shepherd and Overseer of your souls.

The Purpose of the Law

10

○ WEEK 1

● WEEK 2

○ WEEK 3

Galatians 3:19–26

THE PURPOSE OF THE LAW

¹⁹ Why then was the law given? It was added for the sake of transgressions until the Seed to whom the promise was made would come. The law was put into effect through angels by means of a mediator. ²⁰ Now a mediator is not just for one person alone, but God is one. ²¹ Is the law therefore contrary to God's promises? Absolutely not! For if the law had been granted with the ability to give life, then righteousness would certainly be on the basis of the law. ²² But the Scripture imprisoned everything under sin's power, so that the promise might be given on the basis of faith in Jesus Christ to those who believe. ²³ Before this faith came, we were confined under the law, imprisoned until the coming faith was revealed. ²⁴ The law, then, was our guardian until Christ, so that we could be justified by faith. ²⁵ But since that faith has come, we are no longer under a guardian, ²⁶ for through faith you are all sons of God in Christ Jesus.

Jeremiah 31:31–34

THE NEW COVENANT

[31] "Look, the days are coming"—this is the Lord's declaration—"when I will make a new covenant with the house of Israel and with the house of Judah. [32] This one will not be like the covenant I made with their ancestors on the day I took them by the hand to lead them out of the land of Egypt—my covenant that they broke even though I am their master"—the Lord's declaration. [33] "Instead, this is the covenant I will make with the house of Israel after those days"—the Lord's declaration. "I will put my teaching within them and write it on their hearts. I will be their God, and they will be my people. [34] No longer will one teach his neighbor or his brother, saying, 'Know the Lord,' for they will all know me, from the least to the greatest of them"—this is the Lord's declaration. "For I will forgive their iniquity and never again remember their sin."

Romans 3:21–26

THE RIGHTEOUSNESS OF GOD THROUGH FAITH

[21] But now, apart from the law, the righteousness of God has been revealed, attested by the Law and the Prophets. [22] The righteousness of God is through faith in Jesus Christ to all who believe, since there is no distinction. [23] For all have sinned and fall short of the glory of God.

[24] They are justified freely by his grace through the redemption that is in Christ Jesus.

[25] God presented him as an atoning sacrifice in his blood, received through faith, to demonstrate his righteousness, because in his restraint God passed over the sins previously committed. [26] God presented him to demonstrate his righteousness at the present time, so that he would be righteous and declare righteous the one who has faith in Jesus.

Hebrews 10:1–10

THE PERFECT SACRIFICE

[1] Since the law has only a shadow of the good things to come, and not the reality itself of those things, it can never perfect the worshipers by the same sacrifices they continually offer year after year. [2] Otherwise, wouldn't they have stopped being offered, since the worshipers, purified once and for all, would no longer have any consciousness of sins? [3] But in the sacrifices there is a reminder of sins year after year. [4] For it is impossible for the blood of bulls and goats to take away sins.

[5] Therefore, as he was coming into the world, he said:

> You did not desire sacrifice and offering,
> but you prepared a body for me.
> [6] You did not delight
> in whole burnt offerings and sin offerings.
> [7] Then I said, "See—
> it is written about me
> in the scroll—
> I have come to do your will, O God."

[8] After he says above, You did not desire or delight in sacrifices and offerings, whole burnt offerings and sin offerings (which are offered according to the law), [9] he then says, See, I have come to do your will. He takes away the first to establish the second. [10] By this will, we have been sanctified through the offering of the body of Jesus Christ once for all time.

The Pauline Epistles

B AD 47–49

Paul's first missionary journey, with Barnabas and John Mark

B AD 49

Paul attends Jerusalem Council with Titus and Barnabas

E Emperor Claudius orders all Jews to leave Rome

B AD 49–52

Paul's second missionary journey, with Silas

B AD 34

Paul's conversion

B AD 50

Paul and Silas go to Lystra; Timothy joins them on second missionary journey

Paul, Silas, and Timothy minister in Thessalonica and plant one of the first churches in Europe

AD 50–51

Paul spends eighteen months in Corinth planting a church

Paul's hearing before Corinth's proconsul, Gallio

B AD 33

Crucifixion, resurrection, and ascension of Jesus*

Pentecost

B AD 51

Paul leaves Timothy and Silas in Berea to continue his work

B AD 52–57

Paul's third missionary journey

AD **30**

AD **50**

AD 35–AD 46

AD 50–51

1 & 2 Thessalonians

AD 52

Galatians

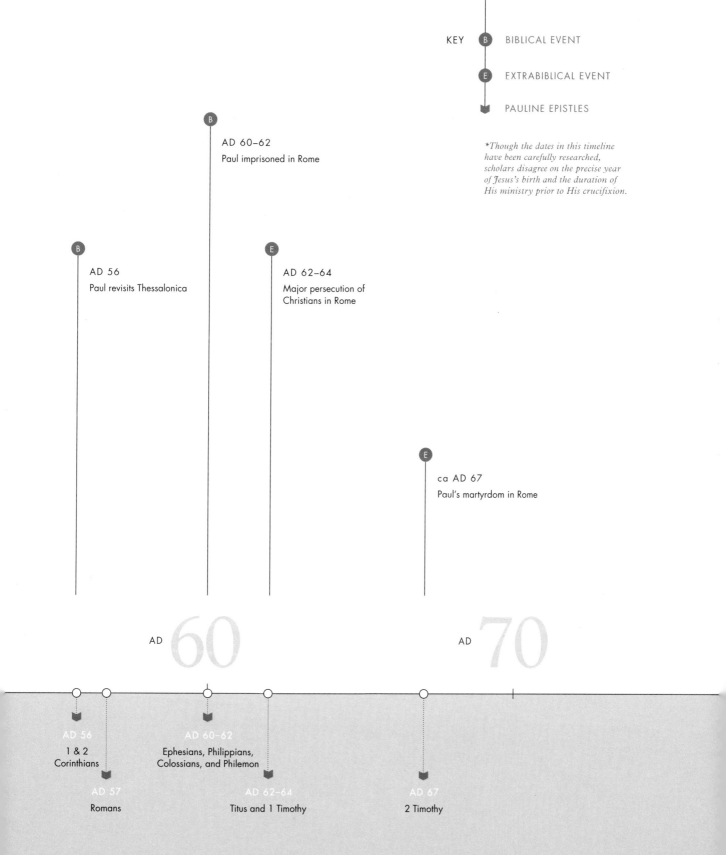

KEY

B BIBLICAL EVENT

E EXTRABIBLICAL EVENT

PAULINE EPISTLES

Though the dates in this timeline have been carefully researched, scholars disagree on the precise year of Jesus's birth and the duration of His ministry prior to His crucifixion.

B

AD 60–62
Paul imprisoned in Rome

B

AD 56
Paul revisits Thessalonica

E

AD 62–64
Major persecution of Christians in Rome

E

ca AD 67
Paul's martyrdom in Rome

AD 60

AD 70

AD 56
1 & 2 Corinthians

AD 57
Romans

AD 60–62
Ephesians, Philippians, Colossians, and Philemon

AD 62–64
Titus and 1 Timothy

AD 67
2 Timothy

God sent the Spirit of his
Son into our hearts, crying,
"Abba, Father!"

GALATIANS 4:6

11 Sons and Heirs

WEEK 1

WEEK 2

WEEK 3

Study questions on p. 72

Galatians 3:27–29

SONS AND HEIRS

27 For those of you who were baptized into Christ have been clothed with Christ. 28 There is no Jew or Greek, slave or free, male and female; since you are all one in Christ Jesus. 29 And if you belong to Christ, then you are Abraham's seed, heirs according to the promise.

Galatians 4:1–7

1 Now I say that as long as the heir is a child, he differs in no way from a slave, though he is the owner of everything. 2 Instead, he is under guardians and trustees until the time set by his father. 3 In the same way we also, when we were children, were in slavery under the elements of the world. 4 When the time came to completion, God sent his Son, born of a woman, born under the law, 5 to redeem those under the law, so that we might receive adoption as sons. 6 And because you are sons, God sent the Spirit of his Son into our hearts, crying, "Abba, Father!" 7 So you are no longer a slave but a son, and if a son, then God has made you an heir.

John 14:1–11, 18–21

THE WAY TO THE FATHER

1 "Don't let your heart be troubled. Believe in God; believe also in me. 2 In my Father's house are many rooms; if not, I would have told you. I am going away to prepare a place for you. 3 If I go away and prepare a place for you, I will come again and take you to myself, so that where I am you may be also. 4 You know the way to where I am going."

5 "Lord," Thomas said, "we don't know where you're going. How can we know the way?"

6 Jesus told him, "I am the way, the truth, and the life. No one comes to the Father except through me. 7 If you know me, you will also know my Father. From now on you do know him and have seen him."

JESUS REVEALS THE FATHER

8 "Lord," said Philip, "show us the Father, and that's enough for us."

9 Jesus said to him, "Have I been among you all this time and you do not know me, Philip? The one who has seen me has seen the Father. How can you say, 'Show us the Father'? 10 Don't you believe that I am in the Father and the Father is in me? The words I speak to you I do not speak on my own. The Father who lives in me does his works. 11 Believe me that I am in the Father and the Father is in me. Otherwise, believe because of the works themselves."

...

THE FATHER, THE SON, AND THE HOLY SPIRIT

18 "I will not leave you as orphans; I am coming to you. 19 In a little while the world will no longer see me, but you will see me. Because I live, you will live too. 20 On that day you will know that I am in my Father, you are in me, and I am in you. 21 The one who has my commands and keeps them is the one who loves me. And the one who loves me will be loved by my Father. I also will love him and will reveal myself to him."

Romans 8:1–17

THE LIFE-GIVING SPIRIT

1 Therefore, there is now no condemnation for those in Christ Jesus, 2 because the law of the Spirit of life in Christ Jesus has set you free from the law of sin and death. 3 What the law could not do since it was weakened by the flesh, God did. He condemned sin in the flesh by sending his own Son in the likeness of sinful flesh as a sin offering, 4 in order that the law's requirement would be fulfilled in us who do not walk according to the flesh but according to the Spirit. 5 For those who live according to the flesh have their minds set on the things of the flesh, but those who live according to the Spirit have their minds set on the things of the Spirit. 6 Now the mind-set of the flesh is death, but the mind-set of the Spirit is life and peace. 7 The mind-set of the flesh is hostile to God because it does not submit to God's law. Indeed, it is unable to do so. 8 Those who are in the flesh cannot please God. 9 You, however, are not in the flesh, but in the Spirit, if indeed the Spirit of God lives in you. If anyone does not have the Spirit of Christ, he does not belong to him. 10 Now if Christ is in you, the body is dead because of sin, but the Spirit gives life because of righteousness. 11 And if the Spirit of him who raised Jesus from the dead lives in you, then he who raised Christ from the dead will also bring your mortal bodies to life through his Spirit who lives in you.

THE HOLY SPIRIT'S MINISTRIES

12 So then, brothers and sisters, we are not obligated to the flesh to live according to the flesh, 13 because if you live according to the flesh, you are going to die. But if by the Spirit you put to death the deeds of the body, you will live. 14 For all those led by God's Spirit are God's sons. 15 For you did not receive a spirit of slavery to fall back into fear. Instead, you received the Spirit of adoption, by whom we cry out, "Abba, Father!" 16 The Spirit himself testifies together with our spirit that we are God's children, 17 and if children, also heirs—heirs of God and coheirs with Christ—if indeed we suffer with him so that we may also be glorified with him.

12 Paul's Concern for the Galatians

WEEK 1

WEEK 2

WEEK 3

Galatians 4:8–20

PAUL'S CONCERN FOR THE GALATIANS

[8] But in the past, since you didn't know God, you were enslaved to things that by nature are not gods. [9] But now, since you know God, or rather have become known by God, how can you turn back again to the weak and worthless elements? Do you want to be enslaved to them all over again? [10] You are observing special days, months, seasons, and years. [11] I am fearful for you, that perhaps my labor for you has been wasted.

[12] I beg you, brothers and sisters: Become like me, for I also became like you. You have not wronged me; [13] you know that previously I preached the gospel to you because of a weakness of the flesh. [14] You did not despise or reject me though my physical condition was a trial for you. On the contrary, you received me as an angel of God, as Christ Jesus himself.

[15] Where, then, is your blessing? For I testify to you that, if possible, you would have torn out your eyes and given them to me. [16] So then, have I become your enemy because I told you the truth? [17] They court you eagerly, but not for good. They want to exclude you from me, so that you would pursue them. [18] But it is always good to be pursued in a good manner—and not just when I am with you. [19] My children, I am again suffering labor pains for you until Christ is formed in you. [20] I would like to be with you right now and change my tone of voice, because I don't know what to do about you.

Deuteronomy 32:1–9

SONG OF MOSES

[1] Pay attention, heavens, and I will speak;
listen, earth, to the words from my mouth.
[2] Let my teaching fall like rain
and my word settle like dew,
like gentle rain on new grass
and showers on tender plants.
[3] For I will proclaim the LORD's name.
Declare the greatness of our God!
[4] The Rock—his work is perfect;
all his ways are just.
A faithful God, without bias,
he is righteous and true.

[5] His people have acted corruptly toward him;
this is their defect—they are not his children
but a devious and crooked generation.
[6] Is this how you repay the LORD,
you foolish and senseless people?
Isn't he your Father and Creator?
Didn't he make you and sustain you?
[7] Remember the days of old;
consider the years of past generations.
Ask your father, and he will tell you,
your elders, and they will teach you.
[8] When the Most High gave the nations their inheritance
and divided the human race,
he set the boundaries of the peoples
according to the number of the people of Israel.
[9] But the LORD's portion is his people,
Jacob, his own inheritance.

Acts 17:24–31

[24] The God who made the world and everything in it—he is Lord of heaven and earth—does not live in shrines made by hands. [25] Neither is he served by human hands, as though he needed anything, since he himself gives everyone life and breath and all things. [26] From one man he has made every nationality to live over the whole earth and has determined their appointed times and the boundaries of where they live.

[27] He did this so that they might seek God, and perhaps they might reach out and find him, though he is not far from each one of us. [28] For in him we live and move and have our being, as even some of your own poets have said, "For we are also his offspring." [29] Since we are God's offspring then, we shouldn't think that the divine nature is like gold or silver or stone, an image fashioned by human art and imagination.

[30] Therefore, having overlooked the times of ignorance, God now commands all people everywhere to repent, [31] because he has set a day when he is going to judge the world in righteousness by the man he has appointed. He has provided proof of this to everyone by raising him from the dead.

Romans 1:18–25

THE GUILT OF THE GENTILE WORLD

[18] For God's wrath is revealed from heaven against all godlessness and unrighteousness of people who by their unrighteousness suppress the truth, [19] since what can be known about God is evident among them, because God has shown it to them. [20] For his invisible attributes, that is, his eternal power and divine nature, have been clearly seen since the creation of the world, being understood through what he has made. As a result, people are without excuse. [21] For though they knew God, they did not glorify him as God or show gratitude. Instead, their thinking became worthless, and their senseless hearts were darkened. [22] Claiming to be wise, they became fools [23] and exchanged the glory of the immortal God for images resembling mortal man, birds, four-footed animals, and reptiles.

[24] Therefore God delivered them over in the desires of their hearts to sexual impurity, so that their bodies were degraded among themselves. [25] They exchanged the truth of God for a lie, and worshiped and served what has been created instead of the Creator, who is praised forever. Amen.

noTes

Creamy Coconut Milk Chai

PREP TIME: 10 MINUTES   COOK TIME: 20 MINUTES   YIELDS: 5 8-OUNCE CUPS

Ingredients

3 cups of water

1 cinnamon stick, broken into pieces

1 tablespoon whole cloves

1 tablespoon cardamom pods

1 teaspoon nutmeg, freshly grated

3 whole star anise

1 teaspoon black peppercorns

1–2 inch piece of fresh ginger, peeled and sliced

4 black tea bags

½ cup real maple syrup

1 15-ounce can unsweetened full-fat coconut milk

Whipped coconut cream

Cinnamon and nutmeg, for garnish

Directions

In a medium pot set over medium heat, bring 3 cups of water to a boil.

Place cinnamon, cloves, cardamom, nutmeg, star anise, and peppercorns in mortar bowl or resealable plastic bag. Crush spices with pestle or using a rolling pin.

Add spice blend, sliced ginger, and tea bags to boiling water.

Reduce heat to low and let simmer for 15 to 20 minutes.

Remove from heat and strain liquid through a mesh strainer into a pitcher. Whisk in maple syrup and coconut milk until creamy.

Serve with whipped coconut cream and dust with cinnamon and nutmeg.

13 GRACE DAY

Use this day to pray, rest, and reflect on this week's reading, giving thanks for the grace that is ours in Christ.

He himself bore our sins in his body on the tree; so that, having died to sins, we might live for righteousness. By his wounds you have been healed.

1 PETER 2:24

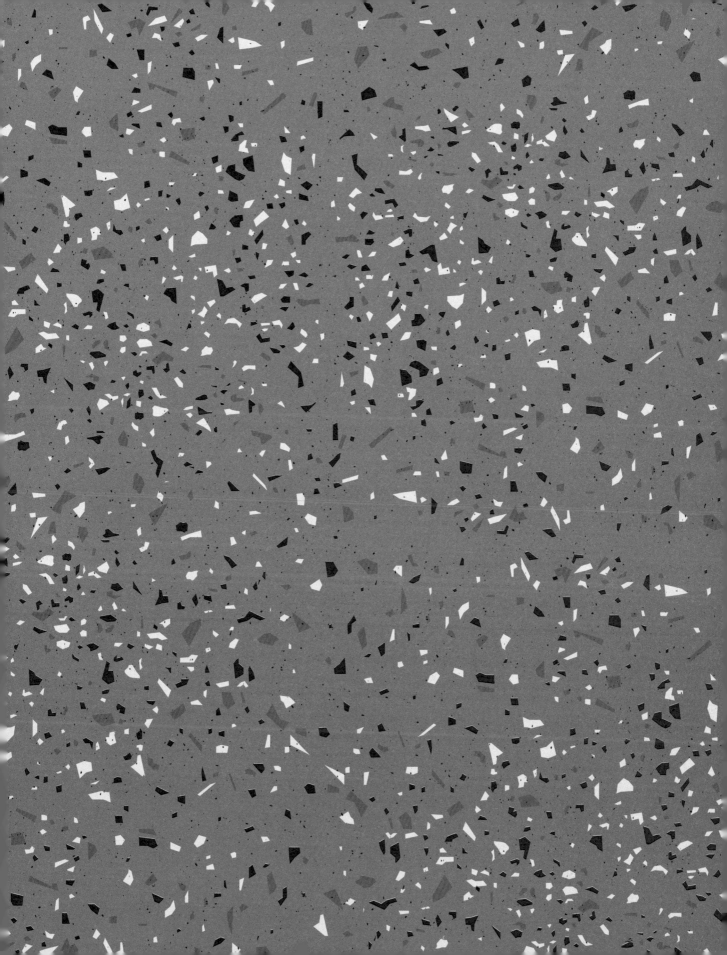

14 WEEKLY TRUTH

Scripture is God-breathed and true. When
we memorize it, we carry the gospel with us
wherever we go.

This week we will memorize a verse from our reading on day 11.
Throughout the book of Galatians, Paul teaches that nothing gives
us an advantage over others in approaching God. Believers have
equal access to God because we are clothed with Christ.

Find the corresponding memory card in the back of this book.

WEEK 1

WEEK 2

WEEK 3

For those of you who were baptized into Christ have been clothed with Christ.

GALATIANS 3:27

Response Questions

Galatians 3:27–29

SONS AND HEIRS

²⁷ For those of you who were baptized into Christ have been clothed with Christ. ²⁸ There is no Jew or Greek, slave or free, male and female; since you are all one in Christ Jesus. ²⁹ And if you belong to Christ, then you are Abraham's seed, heirs according to the promise.

1. Reflect on the passage. What was your immediate reaction upon reading it? Did anything stand out to you?

2. How does Paul's message about equality in Christ affect your life today?

3. Paul says that the gospel is for everyone—that no type of person is better than another in Christ. How should this change how we treat our fellow Christians?

4. How does belonging to Christ change the way you live?

1) Clothed with Him
   -We are all one through Him
   -Everyone is equal

2) Equality ~~brings~~ us together and we need to focus on unity.

3) We treat everyone how we would we would all like to be treated which is a way to live.

4) We can be with Him and live through Him. God keeps us in check through our concients.

Now you too, brothers and
sisters, like Isaac, are children
of promise.

GALATIANS 4:28

15 Sarah and Hagar: Two Covenants

WEEK 1

WEEK 2

WEEK 3

Galatians 4:21–31

SARAH AND HAGAR: TWO COVENANTS

[21] Tell me, you who want to be under the law, don't you hear the law? [22] For it is written that Abraham had two sons, one by a slave and the other by a free woman. [23] But the one by the slave was born as a result of the flesh, while the one by the free woman was born through promise. [24] These things are being taken figuratively, for the women represent two covenants. One is from Mount Sinai and bears children into slavery—this is Hagar. [25] Now Hagar represents Mount Sinai in Arabia and corresponds to the present Jerusalem, for she is in slavery with her children. [26] But the Jerusalem above is free, and she is our mother. [27] For it is written,

> Rejoice, childless woman,
> unable to give birth.
> Burst into song and shout,
> you who are not in labor,
> for the children of the desolate woman will be many,
> more numerous than those
> of the woman who has a husband.

[28] Now you too, brothers and sisters, like Isaac, are children of promise. [29] But just as then the child born as a result of the flesh persecuted the one born as a result of the Spirit, so also now. [30] But what does the Scripture say? "Drive out the slave and her son, for the son of the slave will never be a coheir with the son of the free woman." [31] Therefore, brothers and sisters, we are not children of a slave but of the free woman.

Genesis 16

HAGAR AND ISHMAEL

¹ Abram's wife Sarai had not borne any children for him, but she owned an Egyptian slave named Hagar. ² Sarai said to Abram, "Since the Lord has prevented me from bearing children, go to my slave; perhaps through her I can build a family." And Abram agreed to what Sarai said. ³ So Abram's wife Sarai took Hagar, her Egyptian slave, and gave her to her husband Abram as a wife for him. This happened after Abram had lived in the land of Canaan ten years. ⁴ He slept with Hagar, and she became pregnant. When she saw that she was pregnant, her mistress became contemptible to her. ⁵ Then Sarai said to Abram, "You are responsible for my suffering! I put my slave in your arms, and when she saw that she was pregnant, I became contemptible to her. May the Lord judge between me and you."

⁶ Abram replied to Sarai, "Here, your slave is in your hands; do whatever you want with her." Then Sarai mistreated her so much that she ran away from her.

⁷ The angel of the Lord found her by a spring in the wilderness, the spring on the way to Shur. ⁸ He said, "Hagar, slave of Sarai, where have you come from and where are you going?"

She replied, "I'm running away from my mistress Sarai."

⁹ The angel of the Lord said to her, "Go back to your mistress and submit to her authority." ¹⁰ The angel of the Lord said to her, "I will greatly multiply your offspring, and they will be too many to count."

¹¹ The angel of the Lord said to her, "You have conceived and will have a son. You will name him Ishmael, for the Lord has heard your cry of affliction. ¹² This man will be like a wild donkey. His hand will be against everyone, and everyone's hand will be against him; he will settle near all his relatives."

¹³ So she named the Lord who spoke to her: "You are El-roi," for she said, "In this place, have I actually seen the one who sees me?" ¹⁴ That is why the well is called Beer-lahai-roi. It is between Kadesh and Bered.

¹⁵ So Hagar gave birth to Abram's son, and Abram named his son (whom Hagar bore) Ishmael. ¹⁶ Abram was eighty-six years old when Hagar bore Ishmael to him.

Romans 9:6–8

⁶ Now it is not as though the word of God has failed, because not all who are descended from Israel are Israel. ⁷ Neither are all of Abraham's children his descendants. On the contrary, your offspring will be traced through Isaac. ⁸ That is, it is not the children by physical descent who are God's children, but the children of the promise are considered to be the offspring.

Hebrews 12:18–24

¹⁸ For you have not come to what could be touched, to a blazing fire, to darkness, gloom, and storm, ¹⁹ to the blast of a trumpet, and the sound of words. Those who heard it begged that not another word be spoken to them, ²⁰ for they could not bear what was commanded: If even an animal touches the mountain, it must be stoned. ²¹ The appearance was so terrifying that Moses said, I am trembling with fear. ²² Instead, you have come to Mount Zion, to the city of the living God (the heavenly Jerusalem), to myriads of angels, a festive gathering, ²³ to the assembly of the firstborn whose names have been written in heaven, to a Judge, who is God of all, to the spirits of righteous people made perfect, ²⁴ and to Jesus, the mediator of a new covenant, and to the sprinkled blood, which says better things than the blood of Abel.

Freedom of the Christian

16

WEEK 1

WEEK 2

WEEK 3

Galatians 5:1–15

FREEDOM OF THE CHRISTIAN

[1] For freedom, Christ set us free. Stand firm then and don't submit again to a yoke of slavery. [2] Take note! I, Paul, am telling you that if you get yourselves circumcised, Christ will not benefit you at all. [3] Again I testify to every man who gets himself circumcised that he is obligated to do the entire law. [4] You who are trying to be justified by the law are alienated from Christ; you have fallen from grace. [5] For we eagerly await through the Spirit, by faith, the hope of righteousness. [6] For in Christ Jesus neither circumcision nor uncircumcision accomplishes anything; what matters is faith working through love.

[7] You were running well. Who prevented you from being persuaded regarding the truth? [8] This persuasion does not come from the one who calls you. [9] A little leaven leavens the whole batch of dough. [10] I myself am persuaded in the Lord you will not accept any other view. But whoever it is that is confusing you will pay the penalty. [11] Now brothers and sisters, if I still preach circumcision, why am I still persecuted? In that case the offense of the cross has been abolished. [12] I wish those who are disturbing you might also let themselves be mutilated!

[13] For you were called to be free, brothers and sisters; only don't use this freedom as an opportunity for the flesh, but serve one another through love. [14] For the whole law is fulfilled in one statement: Love your neighbor as yourself. [15] But if you bite and devour one another, watch out, or you will be consumed by one another.

For you were called to be free, brothers
and sisters; only don't use this freedom
as an opportunity for the flesh, but
serve one another through love.

GALATIANS 5:13

Numbers 11:1–20

COMPLAINTS ABOUT HARDSHIP

[1] Now the people began complaining openly before the Lord about hardship. When the Lord heard, his anger burned, and fire from the Lord blazed among them and consumed the outskirts of the camp. [2] Then the people cried out to Moses, and he prayed to the Lord, and the fire died down. [3] So that place was named Taberah, because the Lord's fire had blazed among them.

COMPLAINTS ABOUT FOOD

[4] The riffraff among them had a strong craving for other food. The Israelites wept again and said, "Who will feed us meat? [5] We remember the free fish we ate in Egypt, along with the cucumbers, melons, leeks, onions, and garlic. [6] But now our appetite is gone; there's nothing to look at but this manna!"

[7] The manna resembled coriander seed, and its appearance was like that of bdellium. [8] The people walked around and gathered it. They ground it on a pair of grinding stones or crushed it in a mortar, then boiled it in a cooking pot and shaped it into cakes. It tasted like a pastry cooked with the finest oil. [9] When the dew fell on the camp at night, the manna would fall with it.

[10] Moses heard the people, family after family, weeping at the entrance of their tents. The Lord was very angry; Moses was also provoked. [11] So Moses asked the Lord, "Why have you brought such trouble on your servant? Why are you angry with me, and why do you burden me with all these people? [12] Did I conceive all these people? Did I give them birth so you should tell me, 'Carry them at your breast, as a nanny carries a baby,' to the land that you swore to give their fathers? [13] Where can I get meat to give all these people? For they are weeping to me, 'Give us meat to eat!' [14] I can't carry all these people by myself. They are too much for me. [15] If you are going to treat me like this, please kill me right now if I have found favor with you, and don't let me see my misery anymore."

He gets angry in the Old Testament

Moses had a lot of weigh to carry, he even was stressed like us

SEVENTY ELDERS ANOINTED

[16] The Lord answered Moses, "Bring me seventy men from Israel known to you as elders and officers of the people. Take them to the tent of meeting and have them stand there with you. [17] Then I will come down and speak with you there. I will take some of the Spirit who is on you and put the Spirit on them. They will help you bear the burden of the people, so that you do not have to bear it by yourself.

[18] "Tell the people: Consecrate yourselves in readiness for tomorrow, and you will eat meat because you wept in the Lord's hearing, 'Who will feed us meat? We were better off in Egypt.' The Lord will give you meat and you will eat. [19] You will eat, not for one day, or two days, or five days, or ten days, or twenty days, [20] but for a whole month—until it comes out of your nostrils and becomes

They didn't know what they wanted

nauseating to you—because you have rejected the LORD who is among you, and wept before him: 'Why did we ever leave Egypt?'"

Romans 2:25–29

CIRCUMCISION OF THE HEART

[25] Circumcision benefits you if you observe the law, but if you are a lawbreaker, your circumcision has become uncircumcision. [26] So if an uncircumcised man keeps the law's requirements, will not his uncircumcision be counted as circumcision? [27] A man who is physically uncircumcised, but who keeps the law, will judge you who are a lawbreaker in spite of having the letter of the law and circumcision. [28] For a person is not a Jew who is one outwardly, and true circumcision is not something visible in the flesh. [29] On the contrary, a person is a Jew who is one inwardly, and circumcision is of the heart—by the Spirit, not the letter. That person's praise is not from people but from God.

All is equal now

1 John 3:19–24

[19] This is how we will know that we belong to the truth and will reassure our hearts before him [20] whenever our hearts condemn us;

for God is greater than our hearts, and he knows all things.

[21] Dear friends, if our hearts don't condemn us, we have confidence before God [22] and receive whatever we ask from him because we keep his commands and do what is pleasing in his sight. [23] Now this is his command: that we believe in the name of his Son Jesus Christ, and love one another as he commanded us. [24] The one who keeps his commands remains in him, and he in him. And the way we know that he remains in us is from the Spirit he has given us.

If we live by the Spirit,
let us also keep in step
with the Spirit.

GALATIANS 5:25

The Spirit Versus the Flesh

17

WEEK 1

WEEK 2

WEEK 3

Study questions on p. 98

Galatians 5:16–26

THE SPIRIT VERSUS THE FLESH

[16] I say then, walk by the Spirit and you will certainly not carry out the desire of the flesh. [17] For the flesh desires what is against the Spirit, and the Spirit desires what is against the flesh; these are opposed to each other, so that you don't do what you want. [18] But if you are led by the Spirit, you are not under the law.

[19] Now the works of the flesh are obvious: sexual immorality, moral impurity, promiscuity, [20] idolatry, sorcery, hatreds, strife, jealousy, outbursts of anger, selfish ambitions, dissensions, factions, [21] envy, drunkenness, carousing, and anything similar. I am warning you about these things—as I warned you before—that those who practice such things will not inherit the kingdom of God.

[22] But the fruit of the Spirit is love, joy, peace, patience, kindness, goodness, faithfulness, [23] gentleness, and self-control. The law is not against such things. [24] Now those who belong to Christ Jesus have crucified the flesh with its passions and desires. [25] If we live by the Spirit, let us also keep in step with the Spirit. [26] Let us not become conceited, provoking one another, envying one another.

Ezekiel 37:1–14

THE VALLEY OF DRY BONES

¹ The hand of the LORD was on me, and he brought me out by his Spirit and set me down in the middle of the valley; it was full of bones. ² He led me all around them. There were a great many of them on the surface of the valley, and they were very dry. ³ Then he said to me, "Son of man, can these bones live?"

I replied, "Lord GOD, only you know."

⁴ He said to me, "Prophesy concerning these bones and say to them: Dry bones, hear the word of the LORD! ⁵ This is what the Lord GOD says to these bones: I will cause breath to enter you, and you will live. ⁶ I will put tendons on you, make flesh grow on you, and cover you with skin. I will put breath in you so that you come to life. Then you will know that I am the LORD."

⁷ So I prophesied as I had been commanded. While I was prophesying, there was a noise, a rattling sound, and the bones came together, bone to bone. ⁸ As I looked, tendons appeared on them, flesh grew, and skin covered them, but there was no breath in them. ⁹ He said to me, "Prophesy to the breath, prophesy, son of man. Say to it: This is what the Lord GOD says: Breath, come from the four winds and breathe into these slain so that they may live!" ¹⁰ So I prophesied as he commanded me; the breath entered them, and they came to life and stood on their feet, a vast army.

¹¹ Then he said to me, "Son of man, these bones are the whole house of Israel. Look how they say, 'Our bones are dried up, and our hope has perished; we are cut off.' ¹² Therefore, prophesy and say to them: 'This is what the Lord GOD says: I am going to open your graves and bring you up from them, my people, and lead you into the land of Israel. ¹³ You will know that I am the LORD, my people, when I open your graves and bring you up from them. ¹⁴ I will put my Spirit in you, and you will live, and I will settle you in your own land. Then you will know that I am the LORD. I have spoken, and I will do it. This is the declaration of the LORD.'"

Ephesians 2:1–10

FROM DEATH TO LIFE

¹ And you were dead in your trespasses and sins ² in which you previously lived according to the ways of this world, according to the ruler of the power of the air, the spirit now working in the disobedient. ³ We too all previously lived among them in our fleshly desires, carrying out the inclinations of our flesh and thoughts, and we were by nature children under wrath as the others were also. ⁴ But God, who is rich in mercy, because of his great love that he had for us, ⁵ made us alive with Christ even though we were dead in trespasses. You are saved by grace! ⁶ He also raised us up with him and seated us with him in the heavens in Christ Jesus,

[7] so that in the coming ages he might display the immeasurable riches of his grace through his kindness to us in Christ Jesus. [8] For you are saved by grace through faith, and this is not from yourselves; it is God's gift— [9] not from works, so that no one can boast. [10] For we are his workmanship, created in Christ Jesus for good works, which God prepared ahead of time for us to do.

Revelation 21:1–8

THE NEW CREATION

[1] Then I saw a new heaven and a new earth; for the first heaven and the first earth had passed away, and the sea was no more. [2] I also saw the holy city, the new Jerusalem, coming down out of heaven from God, prepared like a bride adorned for her husband.

[3] Then I heard a loud voice from the throne: Look, God's dwelling is with humanity, and he will live with them. They will be his peoples, and God himself will be with them and will be their God. [4] He will wipe away every tear from their eyes. Death will be no more; grief, crying, and pain will be no more, because the previous things have passed away.

[5] Then the one seated on the throne said, "Look, I am making everything new." He also said, "Write, because these words are faithful and true." [6] Then he said to me, "It is done! I am the Alpha and the Omega, the beginning and the end. I will freely give to the thirsty from the spring of the water of life. [7] The one who conquers will inherit these things, and I will be his God, and he will be my son. [8] But the cowards, faithless, detestable, murderers, sexually immoral, sorcerers, idolaters, and all liars—their share will be in the lake that burns with fire and sulfur, which is the second death."

Fruit

OF THE

Spirit

Paul's illustration of the fruit of the Spirit in Galatians 5 calls to mind Jesus's metaphor of the vine and the branches in John 15. Jesus said to His disciples, "I am the vine; you are the branches. The one who remains in me and I in him produces much fruit, because you can do nothing without me" (Jn 15:5).

Here is the fruit of the Spirit listed in Galatians 5:22–23, along with definitions and other key references.

FRUIT OF THE SPIRIT IN ENGLISH AND GREEK	DEFINITION	OTHER KEY REFERENCES
Love *Agape*	Self-giving for the highest good of others. Unconditional commitment.	JN 15:12–14 RM 13:10 1CO 13 EPH 5:25
Joy *Chara*	Delight. Gladness. A divine expression of the Spirit's presence.	RM 14:17 1PT 1:8–9
Peace *Eirene*	Harmony between individuals and groups. Life-sustaining unity.	RM 5:1 PHP 4:7 COL 3:15
Patience *Makrothymia*	Steadfastness. Longsuffering. Bearing burdens and trials without complaining.	1CO 13:4 COL 1:11; 3:12 1TH 5:14–15
Kindness *Chrestotes*	Gracious actions and attitude toward imperfect people. Mercy. Uprightness.	RM 2:4 EPH 2:7 TI 3:4
Goodness *Agathosyne*	Generosity. Usefulness. Moral excellence.	RM 15:14 EPH 5:8–9
Faithfulness *Pistis*	Trustworthy. Reliable. Acts on conviction.	RM 3:3 TI 3:8 RV 2:10
Gentleness *Praotes*	Meekness. Humble disposition toward God's will. Not aggressive or driven by anger.	TI 3:1–2 1PT 3:15–16
Self-Control *Egkrateia*	Restraint of emotions, actions, and desires, in order to be in harmony with God's will. Self-sacrificing.	TI 2:11–12 2PT 1:5–6

Though we tend to talk about the fruit of the Spirit as multiple fruits, in the original Greek of Galatians, fruit is singular. Love, joy, peace, patience, kindness, goodness, faithfulness, gentleness, and self-control are all aspects of the fruit that comes with walking in the ways of the Spirit.

Carry One Another's Burdens

18

WEEK 1

WEEK 2

WEEK 3

Galatians 6:1–10

CARRY ONE ANOTHER'S BURDENS

¹ Brothers and sisters, if someone is overtaken in any wrongdoing, you who are spiritual, restore such a person with a gentle spirit, watching out for yourselves so that you also won't be tempted. ² Carry one another's burdens; in this way you will fulfill the law of Christ. ³ For if anyone considers himself to be something when he is nothing, he deceives himself. ⁴ Let each person examine his own work, and then he can take pride in himself alone, and not compare himself with someone else. ⁵ For each person will have to carry his own load.

⁶ Let the one who is taught the word share all his good things with the teacher. ⁷ Don't be deceived: God is not mocked. For whatever a person sows he will also reap, ⁸ because the one who sows to his flesh will reap destruction from the flesh, but the one who sows to the Spirit will reap eternal life from the Spirit. ⁹ Let us not get tired of doing good, for we will reap at the proper time if we don't give up. ¹⁰ Therefore, as we have opportunity, let us work for the good of all, especially for those who belong to the household of faith.

Hosea 10:12

Sow righteousness for yourselves
and reap faithful love;
break up your unplowed ground.
It is time to seek the LORD
until he comes and sends righteousness
on you like the rain.

John 15:9–17

CHRISTLIKE LOVE

9 "As the Father has loved me, I have also loved you. Remain in my love. 10 If you keep my commands you will remain in my love, just as I have kept my Father's commands and remain in his love.

11 "I have told you these things so that my joy may be in you and your joy may be complete.

12 "This is my command: Love one another as I have loved you. 13 No one has greater love than this: to lay down his life for his friends. 14 You are my friends if you do what I command you. 15 I do not call you servants anymore, because a servant doesn't know what his master is doing. I have called you friends, because I have made known to you everything I have heard from my Father. 16 You did not choose me, but I chose you. I appointed you to go and produce fruit and that your fruit should remain, so that whatever you ask the Father in my name, he will give you.

17 "This is what I command you: Love one another."

James 2:14–26

FAITH AND WORKS

14 What good is it, my brothers and sisters, if someone claims to have faith but does not have works? Can such faith save him? 15 If a brother or sister is without clothes and lacks daily food 16 and one of you says to them, "Go in peace, stay warm, and be well fed," but you don't give them what the body needs, what good is it? 17 In the same way faith, if it doesn't have works, is dead by itself.

18 But someone will say, "You have faith, and I have works." Show me your faith without works, and I will show you faith by my works. 19 You believe that God is one. Good! Even the demons believe—and they shudder.

20 Senseless person! Are you willing to learn that faith without works is useless? 21 Wasn't Abraham our father justified by works in offering Isaac his son on the altar? 22 You see that faith was active together with his works, and by works, faith was made complete, 23 and the Scripture was fulfilled that says, Abraham believed God, and it was credited to him as righteousness, and he was called God's friend. 24 You see that a person is justified by works and not by faith alone. 25 In the same way, wasn't Rahab the prostitute also justified by works in receiving the messengers and sending them out by a different route? 26 For just as the body without the spirit is dead, so also faith without works is dead.

19 Concluding Exhortation

WEEK 1

WEEK 2

WEEK 3

Galatians 6:11–18

CONCLUDING EXHORTATION

[11] Look at what large letters I use as I write to you in my own handwriting. [12] Those who want to make a good impression in the flesh are the ones who would compel you to be circumcised—but only to avoid being persecuted for the cross of Christ. [13] For even the circumcised don't keep the law themselves, and yet they want you to be circumcised in order to boast about your flesh. [14] But as for me, I will never boast about anything except the cross of our Lord Jesus Christ. The world has been crucified to me through the cross, and I to the world. [15] For both circumcision and uncircumcision mean nothing; what matters instead is a new creation. [16] May peace come to all those who follow this standard, and mercy even to the Israel of God!

[17] From now on, let no one cause me trouble, because I bear on my body the marks of Jesus. [18] Brothers and sisters, the grace of our Lord Jesus Christ be with your spirit. Amen.

Brothers and sisters, the grace of our
Lord Jesus Christ be with your spirit.
Amen.

GALATIANS 6:18

Jeremiah 9:23–24

BOAST IN THE LORD

²³ "This is what the LORD says:

The wise person should not boast in his wisdom;
the strong should not boast in his strength;
the wealthy should not boast in his wealth.
²⁴ But the one who boasts should boast in this:
that he understands and knows me—
that I am the LORD, showing faithful love,
justice, and righteousness on the earth,
for I delight in these things.
This is the LORD's declaration."

Matthew 23:1–36

RELIGIOUS HYPOCRITES DENOUNCED

¹ Then Jesus spoke to the crowds and to his disciples: ² "The scribes and the Pharisees are seated in the chair of Moses. ³ Therefore do whatever they tell you, and observe it. But don't do what they do, because they don't practice what they teach. ⁴ They tie up heavy loads that are hard to carry and put them on people's shoulders, but they themselves aren't willing to lift a finger to move them. ⁵ They do everything to be seen by others: They enlarge their phylacteries and lengthen their tassels. ⁶ They love the place of honor at banquets, the front seats in the synagogues, ⁷ greetings in the marketplaces, and to be called 'Rabbi' by people.

⁸ "But you are not to be called 'Rabbi,' because you have one Teacher, and you are all brothers and sisters. ⁹ Do not call anyone on earth your father, because you have one Father, who is in heaven. ¹⁰ You are not to be called instructors either, because you have one Instructor, the Messiah. ¹¹ The greatest among you will be your servant. ¹² Whoever exalts himself will be humbled, and whoever humbles himself will be exalted.

¹³ "Woe to you, scribes and Pharisees, hypocrites! You shut the door of the kingdom of heaven in people's faces. For you don't go in, and you don't allow those entering to go in.

¹⁵ "Woe to you, scribes and Pharisees, hypocrites! You travel over land and sea to make one convert, and when he becomes one, you make him twice as fit for hell as you are!

¹⁶ "Woe to you, blind guides, who say, 'Whoever takes an oath by the temple, it means nothing. But whoever takes an oath by the gold of the temple is bound by his oath.' ¹⁷ Blind fools! For which is greater, the gold or the temple that sanctified the gold? ¹⁸ Also, 'Whoever takes an oath by the altar, it means nothing; but whoever takes an oath by the gift that is on it is bound by his oath.' ¹⁹ Blind people! For which is greater, the gift or the altar that sanctifies the gift? ²⁰ Therefore, the one who takes an oath by the altar takes an oath by it and by everything on it. ²¹ The one who takes an oath by the temple takes an oath by it and by him who dwells in it. ²² And the one who takes an oath by heaven takes an oath by God's throne and by him who sits on it.

²³ "Woe to you, scribes and Pharisees, hypocrites! You pay a tenth of mint, dill, and cumin, and yet you have neglected the more important matters of the law—justice, mercy, and faithfulness. These things should have been done without neglecting the others. ²⁴ Blind guides! You strain out a gnat, but gulp down a camel!

²⁵ "Woe to you, scribes and Pharisees, hypocrites! You clean the outside of the cup and dish, but inside they are full of greed and self-indulgence. ²⁶ Blind Pharisee! First clean the inside of the cup, so that the outside of it may also become clean.

²⁷ "Woe to you, scribes and Pharisees, hypocrites! You are like whitewashed tombs, which appear beautiful on the outside, but inside are full of the bones of the dead and every kind of impurity. ²⁸ In the same way, on the outside you seem righteous to people, but inside you are full of hypocrisy and lawlessness.

²⁹ "Woe to you, scribes and Pharisees, hypocrites! You build the tombs of the prophets and decorate the graves of the righteous, ³⁰ and you say, 'If we had lived in the days of our ancestors, we wouldn't have taken part with them in shedding the prophets' blood.' ³¹ So you testify against yourselves that

you are descendants of those who murdered the prophets. ³² Fill up, then, the measure of your ancestors' sins!

³³ "Snakes! Brood of vipers! How can you escape being condemned to hell? ³⁴ This is why I am sending you prophets, sages, and scribes. Some of them you will kill and crucify, and some of them you will flog in your synagogues and pursue from town to town. ³⁵ So all the righteous blood shed on the earth will be charged to you, from the blood of righteous Abel to the blood of Zechariah, son of Berechiah, whom you murdered between the sanctuary and the altar. ³⁶ Truly I tell you, all these things will come on this generation."

2 Corinthians 5:17–21

¹⁷ Therefore, if anyone is in Christ, he is a new creation; the old has passed away, and see, the new has come! ¹⁸ Everything is from God, who has reconciled us to himself through Christ and has given us the ministry of reconciliation. ¹⁹ That is, in Christ, God was reconciling the world to himself, not counting their trespasses against them, and he has committed the message of reconciliation to us.

²⁰ Therefore, we are ambassadors for Christ, since God is making his appeal through us. We plead on Christ's behalf: "Be reconciled to God." ²¹ He made the one who did not know sin to be sin for us, so that in him we might become the righteousness of God.

20 GRACE DAY

Use this day to pray, rest, and reflect on this week's reading, giving thanks for the grace that is ours in Christ.

Sow righteousness for yourselves and reap faithful love; break up your unplowed ground. It is time to seek the LORD until he comes and sends righteousness on you like the rain.

HOSEA 10:12

21 WEEKLY TRUTH

Scripture is God-breathed and true. When
we memorize it, we carry the gospel with us
wherever we go.

Throughout Paul's letter to the Galatians, he encourages believers
to walk in the Spirit. This week, we'll memorize Galatians 5:22–
23, a non-exhaustive list of qualities cultivated in believers as we
follow Jesus.

Find the corresponding memory card in the back of this book.

WEEK 1

WEEK 2

WEEK 3

But the fruit of the Spirit is love, joy, peace, patience, kindness, goodness, faithfulness, gentleness, and self-control.

GALATIANS 5:22–23

WEEK 3 # Response Questions

Galatians 5:22–26

[22] But the fruit of the Spirit is love, joy, peace, patience, kindness, goodness, faithfulness, [23] gentleness, and self-control. The law is not against such things. [24] Now those who belong to Christ Jesus have crucified the flesh with its passions and desires. [25] If we live by the Spirit, let us also keep in step with the Spirit. [26] Let us not become conceited, provoking one another, envying one another.

1. Reflect on the passage. What was your immediate reaction upon reading it? Did anything stand out to you?

2. Which aspect of the fruit of the Spirit is most difficult for you to practice in your daily life?

3. What would it look like to "keep in step with the Spirit"?

1) Don't provoke one another to anger

2) Self-control is the hardest, I need everything at the time I see it, I don't have self control.

3) You live in line with the spirit if you keep all of these things you always have to make sure you are trying your best to be truthful to you and making good decision that get you further in heaven and not the world.

SHE READS TRUTH *is a worldwide community of women who read God's Word together every day.*

Founded in 2012, She Reads Truth invites women of all ages to engage with Scripture through daily reading plans, online conversation led by a vibrant community of contributors, and offline resources created at the intersection of beauty, goodness, and Truth.

SHE READS TRUTH

READY FOR YOUR NEXT READ AFTER GALATIANS?

We have more reading plans that dive deeper into Paul's letters!

Romans walks us through the origin of sin and guilt, the impossibility of saving ourselves, and our ultimate rescue in Christ. **1 & 2 Corinthians** explore what it means to be the body of Christ. **1 & 2 Timothy and Titus** are given to guide young pastors and their congregations on a journey that is faithful and true to the heritage of the gospel of Christ.

ORDER AT SHOPSHEREADSTRUTH.COM

Why Did Paul Write This Letter to the Romans?

I   II

DESIRE

It was Paul's long-time goal to bring the gospel to Rome.

ROMANS 1:9-12

CARE

Paul heard tensions existed between Jewish and Gentile believers in Rome. They lacked a doctrinal foundation to sort out their differences. Paul wanted to address these issues that divided them.

ROMANS 9:30-10:4

Kate Lemmon, 2016. Via Microsoft.

WHERE DID I STUDY?

O HOME
O OFFICE
O COFFEE SHOP
O CHURCH
O A FRIEND'S HOUSE
O OTHER

WHAT WAS I LISTENING TO?

ARTIST:

SONG:

PLAYLIST:

WHEN DID I STUDY?

MORNING

AFTERNOON

NIGHT

What did I learn?

WHAT WAS HAPPENING IN MY LIFE?

WHAT WAS HAPPENING IN THE WORLD?

MONTH	DAY	YEAR

END DATE